A Tune A Day

FOR VIOLIN.
BY C. PAUL HERFURTH.

BOOK TWO.

Exclusive distributors:
Music Sales Limited
14-15 Berners Street, London W1T 3LJ, England.
Music Sales Pty Limited
20 Resolution Drive, Caringbah, NSW 2229, Australia.

Order No. BM10298
ISBN 978-0-7119-1592-3

© *Boston Music Company*

BOSTON MUSIC COMPANY.

DISTRIBUTED BY

7777 W. BLUEMOUND RD. P.O. BOX 13819 MILWAUKEE, WI 53213

DICTIONARY OF TERMS AND SIGNS USED IN MUSIC

For volume of tone:

pp —Pianissimo, very soft.
p —Piano, softly.
mp —Mezzo-piano, rather softly.
mf —Mezzo-forte, rather loudly.
f —Forte, loudly.
ff —Fortissimo, very loud.
sf —Sforzando, strong accent. (> ▲)
cresc. —Crescendo, gradually louder. (━━━━)
dim. —Diminuendo, gradually softer. (━━━━)

For tempo (speed):

Largo—Very slow.
Adagio—Slow.
Andante—Rather slow.
Andantino—A little slower than Andante.
Moderato—Moderately fast.
Allegretto—Lively, but not too fast.
Allegro—Fast.
Vivace—Faster than Allegro.
Presto—Very fast.

For increasing tempo:

Accelerando (Accel.)—Gradually faster.
Stringendo (String.)—Suddenly faster.
Più mosso—A steady, faster speed.

For decreasing tempo:

Rallentando (Rall.)—Gradually slower.
Ritardando (Rit.)—Gradually slower.
Meno mosso—A steady, slower speed.

For style:

Animato—With spirit, with animation.
Agitato—Agitated.
Allargando—Broader.
Cantabile—In a singing style.
Dolce—Sweetly, softly.
Espressivo—With expression.
Legato—Smoothly, connected.
Maestoso—Majestically.
Con Spirito—With spirit.
Staccato—Detached, separated. (ᵛ)
Tenuto—Sustained. (━)
A Tempo—In the original time.

Other signs:

D. C. Da Capo—From the beginning.
Fine (fee-nay)—Ending.
D. S. Dal Segno—Go back to the sign. (𝄋)
Pause (fermata)—Prolongs the time of a note or rest. (𝄐)

TO THE STUDENT

Having completed the study of Book I, you should be thoroughly familiar with the fundamentals of violin playing, such as a good position, correct use of the fingers when placing the left hand, and the elementary principles of bow control.

Book II includes a continuation of the elementary material, presenting slightly more advanced exercises and pieces. To be better able to play the familiar melodies and pieces, it is recommended that you prepare the purely technical exercises at the beginning of each lesson where a new key and finger-placing is introduced.

Study carefully the diagrams introducing additional keys and fingerings when positioning your fingers for the new notes. Remember that you must first read the note and then place the finger, so verify the note you are reading and the exact finger-position for that note. The surest way to play well derives from the ability to read well.

Foster the habit of quick thinking by assimilating the following points *at first glance:*

     (1)   Name of Note (Natural, Sharp or Flat).

     (2)   How to Play (Finger-Position and String).

     (3)   How Long to Hold (Time-Value).

Training your perceptive powers to respond in this manner will enhance your command of violin technique and, correspondingly, enlarge your musical horizon.

Many of my pupils have formed groups which meet to play the duets, trios and quartets with piano, thus forming a little orchestra. Why don't you try it?—you'll have lots of fun!

TO THE TEACHER

In compiling Book II, I have tried to carry out in slightly more advanced material the basic principles of violin playing as laid down in Book I.

The material has been selected and the grading edited to provide sequential progress as each step is mastered. Adequate preparation for the development of the student is allowed for, although the amount of purely technical work has been kept to a minimum. This book is very largely made up of folksongs and other familiar melodies of good musical quality arranged in duet, trio and quartet form, from which the pupil should achieve a sound bowing style and firm grasp of finger—(intonation) technique. An awareness of musical form and harmonic structure stems naturally from the study of these pieces.

The use of the piano accompaniment has proved of value both in the classroom and in the home. That important advantages result from its use is certain. The interest and ambition of the pupil is stimulated by the addition of the harmonic structure, which also serves as a guide to the proper placing of the fingers through hearing the note he is producing in the harmony. The use of the piano part is recommended from the earliest stages so as to stimulate the musical ear to a keen perception of modulations and harmonies, for which the violin, in that particular regard, is comparatively imperfect.

I wish to acknowledge my indebtedness to Mr. Edmund Schill, Director of Music, Verona, N.J., and to Mr. Francis Rice, Teacher of violin classes in East Orange, and Roselle Park, N.J., for their helpful suggestions and criticisms in compiling this series of books.

C. Paul Herfurth.

LESSON 1

Review of Keys Studied in Book 1

LESSON 2
Studies for the use of the second finger in different positions
Two new notes, C natural on the A string and G natural on the E string

The importance of being able to read notes as well as you can read the letters of the alphabet cannot be overestimated. This is the foundation on which your future progress depends. You must also know the exact position of your fingers on the fingerboard so as to be able to play any given note; for example, to play C♯ on the A string, the second finger is placed a whole tone from the first (high position) but to play C natural, the second finger is placed close to the first (low position) Therefore, the necessity of knowing whether the note is natural, sharp or flat is perfectly obvious.

Have a picture of the fingerboard in your mind in order to see where your fingers are placed for the different notes.

Study the following diagram showing position of notes already studied and the two new notes to be taken in this lesson. Name the whole tones and semitones.

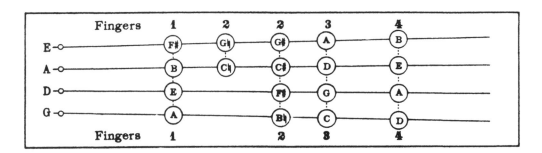

Name the following notes, finger used, high or low position for second finger, and on what string played.

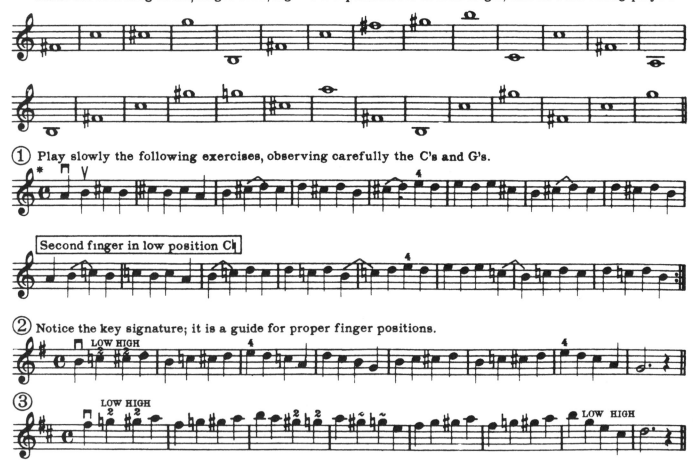

① Play slowly the following exercises, observing carefully the C's and G's.

Second finger in low position C♮

② Notice the key signature; it is a guide for proper finger positions.

LOW HIGH

③ LOW HIGH

*Exercise No. 1 may also be played on the E string.

LESSON 3
Familiar Melodies Using The Second Finger in the Low Position

Lightly Row

The First Noël

Home, Sweet Home

Henry R. Bishop
1783 - 1855

*Advanced pupils may also play the teacher parts.

LESSON 4
G Major Scale and Arpeggio in Two Octaves

Duet

God Save The Queen

Attributed to Henry Carey
1690-1743

Little Study

Franz Wohlfahrt
1823-1884

Home work. Mark with this sign ∧ the half steps in both parts of exercise No. 4. Write 4 times the G Major scale in 2 octaves marking the half steps and placing the sharp. Manuscript sheet page 7.

LESSON 5

Continuation of the key of G
Exercises in crossing from C natural to F#

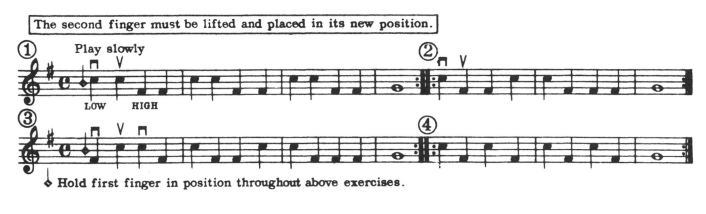

The second finger must be lifted and placed in its new position.

♦ Hold first finger in position throughout above exercises.

Duet

Practise both parts.

Hohmann

Little Waltz

Hohmann

Tempo Waltz (In waltz time)

Home work: Mark half steps on this page the same as before.

LESSON 6

Flow Gently, Sweet Afton
(Quartet)

James E. Spilman

Andante (Slowly)

Pupil

Pupil

Pupil

Teacher

Evening Song

Robert Schumann
1810 - 1856

Moderato (Moderately fast)

Pupil

Teacher

rit., abbreviation for ritenuto— gradually slackening in speed.

Note: **All** manuscript pages are to be **used for** home-work according to instructions.

LESSON 7

Two new notes, F natural on the D string and B flat on the G string. Study the following diagram so as to *visualize* the exact position of these two notes upon the fingerboard.

Practise both parts on the double staff in this and the following lessons.

C Major Scale

⑦ Play also as crotchets, separate and slurred bowing. Learn to spell each new scale.

Softly Now the Light of Day

Carl Maria von Weber
1786 - 1826

⑧ Andante (Slowly)

Pupil

Pupil

Home work: Write C Major scale 4 times, marking the half steps. Also fill in blanks in above diagram.

Learn to take particular notice of the key signature before playing.

America, the Beautiful

Samuel A. Ward
1847-1908

Go Down, Moses

Follow the bowings carefully

Andante (Slowly)

Negro Spiritual

Home work: Mark the half steps on this page.

LESSON 9
Continuation of the key of C Major

In scale passages use the open string in ascending, and the fourth finger in descending.

Russian Hymn

Lento (Very slowly)

Home work: Mark the half steps on this page as before.

LESSON 10

Onward, Christian Soldiers
Trio

Sir Arthur Sullivan
1842-1900

Moderato (Moderately fast)

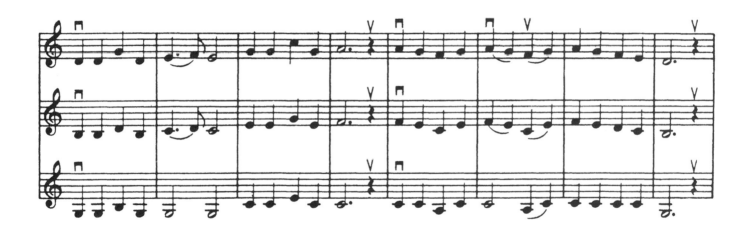

LESSON 11

Note carefully the key signatures and what they mean.

D. C.— Da Capo— to beginning.

Fine— End

Melody
Trio

Franz Joseph Haydn
1732-1809

English Morris Dance

Melody

Ludwig van Beethoven
1770 -1827

LESSON 12
Christmas Carols

Theme From "Lobgesang"

Felix Mendelssohn Bartholdy
1809 - 1847

O Come, All Ye Faithful
(Adeste Fideles)

XIIIth Century Latin Hymn

Silent Night, Holy Night

Franz Gruber
1787 - 1863

In this and lesson **16**, two new notes are taken up. F♮ on the E string and B♭ on the A string, to be played with the **1st** finger placed close to the nut. Study diagram to see position of notes on the fingerboard. Great care must be taken in playing these notes. *Do not allow the knuckle at the base of the first finger to slide under the neck.* Play with the tips of the fingers.

Little Scale Study

Duet

Home work: Mark the half steps in this lesson and fill in blanks in above diagram.

Continuation of the key of C Major using F natural on the E string.

Long, Long Ago

Thomas H. Bayly

Duet

Jacques Féréol Mazas
1782-1849

Home work: Mark half steps in this lesson.

*D. S. Dal Segno— Back to the sign. (𝄋)

LESSON 15

The Little Sandman

Johannes Brahms
1833-1897

Theme from Symphony No. 11
(Military Symphony)

Haydn

First and Second Time Bar

The term 1st and 2nd time bars applies to one or more bars in brackets at a double bar; thus when the strain is repeated, the first time bar is omitted and the second time bar played instead.

German College Song

LESSON 16
Key of F Major

Key of F Major, one flat (♭). The flat (♭) placed on the third line of the staff, just after the clef sign, affects every B throughout the piece. Refer to diagram in Lesson 13 to see the exact position of this note on the fingerboard.

Scale and Arpeggio of F Major
Half Steps A to B♭ and E to F

Deck the Hall

Old Welsh

Home work: Mark half steps. Write F Major scale 4 times.

LESSON 17
Continuation of the key of F Major

All Through the Night

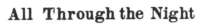

Santa Lucia

Little Study in F

*Andantino _ Slower than Andante.

LESSON 18
Six-eight time

Count six beats to each bar in slow tempo a quaver (♪) being the unit of a beat.
Count two beats to each bar in fast tempo a dotted crotchet (♩.) being the unit of beat.

Preparatory exercise. Repeat each of the following bars until the rhythm of the different groupings is memorized. Play on the open strings. *Count aloud*

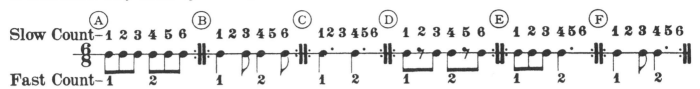

Notice key signature and finger accordingly.
Play exercises slowly at first, gradually increasing the speed.

Play the D Major scale different ways using the various rhythm patterns indicated above.

Row, Row, Row Your Boat

The above tune may be used as a round by dividing the class into two or four groups.

Peek - A - Boo

Allegro (*Brightly*)   C. P. H.

Oh Dear! What Can the Matter Be?

⑥ Allegretto   English Folk Song

Home work: Write 4 lines of notes, using different groupings in ⁶⁄₈ time dividing into bars.

LESSON 19
Detached notes of different values in one bow

Bowing drill: Practise this line carefully, gradually increasing the speed.

Oats and Beans

Allegretto (brightly)

Old English

Mulberry Bush

Allegretto

English Folk Song

*Ding - Dong

Allegretto

B. Remick.

Wee Willie Winkie

Allegretto

C.P.H.

Old English Morris Dance

Allegretto

* Used by permission of Silver-Burdett Co. Morristown. N.J. U.S.A.

Continuation of $\frac{6}{8}$ time

Drink To Me Only With Thine Eyes

Old English Air

It Came Upon a Midnight Clear

Richard S. Willis
1819–1900

Scale Study

*Place finger on both strings at once.

22

Note: All manuscript pages are to be used for home-work according to instructions.

Key of B♭ Major

Key of B♭. B♭ and E♭. See diagram for position of E♭ on the D string. Review position of B♭ on the G string in Lesson 7.

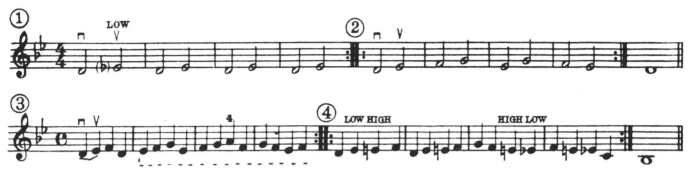

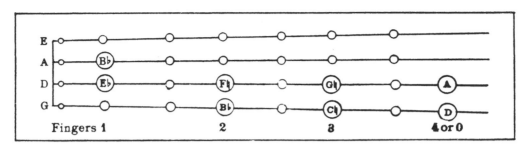

Scale of B♭

⑤ Half steps D to E♭, and A to B♭.   Play also as crotchets.

Home work: Write the B♭ Major scale 4 times, marking flats and half steps; also fill in blanks in above diagram.

LESSON 22

Vesper Hymn
Trio

Old Russian

Pupil

Pupil

Teacher

A Capital Ship
(Marching Song)

Old English Tune

March time

*a tempo,— as before.

Continuation of the key of B♭ Major

Scale Study

The Blacksmith

Mozart
1756-1791

Moderato

mf

A Little Song

C.P.H.

Allegretto

mf

p

cresc.

rit.

*a tempo***

mf

rit.

rit., abbreviation for ritenuto — gradually slackening in speed.
**a tempo,— as before.

LESSON 24
Scale of B♭ Major, upper octave
Review lower octave of this scale in lesson 21.

Scale of B♭ Major, upper octave
Half steps D to E♭, and A to B♭

Notice that you can not play the open E string.

Scale of B♭ Major, two octaves

The Star-Spangled Banner

Melody "Anacreon in Heaven"
John Stafford Smith
1750–1836

Home work: Write the B♭ Major scale in two octaves 4 times, marking flats and the half steps.

LESSON 25
Key of E♭ Major

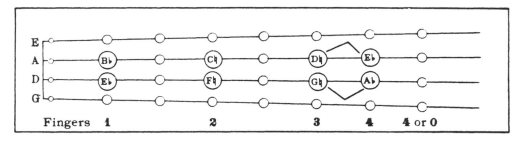

Fingers   1   2   3   4   4 or 0

Scale of E♭ Major – name the flats

Notice that the finger placing is the same as for the upper octave of the B♭ major scale.

Recite the notes of all scales studied.

Use different bowings as in other scales, and play also as crotchets.

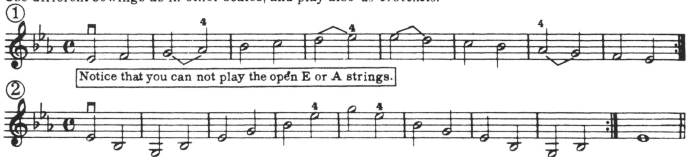

Notice that you can not play the open E or A strings.

Austrian Hymn

Haydn

Home work: Write the E♭ Major scale 4 times, marking as before.

LESSON 26
Key of E Major

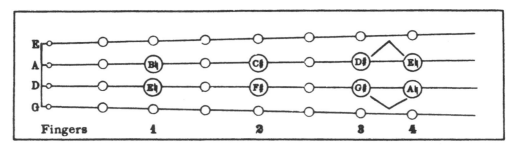

Scale of E Major – name the sharps

Same finger placing as for the E♭ scale, except that each finger is one semitone higher.

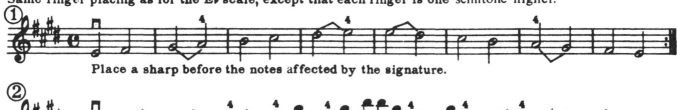

Place a sharp before the notes affected by the signature.

German Folk Song

Cradle Song

Andante   Brahms

Home work: Write the E Major scale 4 times, marking as before.

LESSON 27
Key of A Major

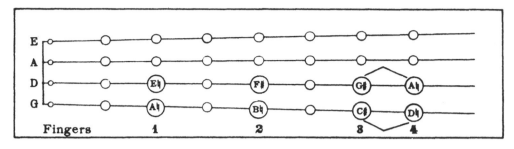

Scale of A Major- name the sharps

Same finger placing as for the E major scale.

Place a sharp before the notes affected by the signature.

Chimes of Dunkirk

Scale of A Major in two octaves

O Worship the King

Haydn

Pupil

Teacher

LESSON 28
Semiquavers

A semiquaver is equal to half the value of a quaver. Two semiquavers equal one quaver and four semiquavers equal one crotchet. Abbreviations for semiquavers.

Comparative table showing number of semiquavers to other notes studied thus far.

Bird Song

Andante

Pupil

Teacher

In this piece, which requires a slow movement, it is better to divide the $\frac{2}{4}$ time into $\frac{4}{8}$ (one count to each quaver)

Kingdom Comin'

Allegretto

Dotted Quavers and Semiquavers
Legato (Connected)

This is one of the more difficult rhythms to learn. The dotted quaver is equal to three semiquavers. Always feel a division of four on each beat when playing this rhythm, three on the dotted quaver and one on the semiquaver.

BE SURE TO PLAY THE DOTTED QUAVER LONG ENOUGH AND THE SEMIQUAVER SHORT ENOUGH.

Legato (Connected)

Largo

(New World Symphony)
Trio

Anton Dvořák
1841-1904

LESSON 30
Dotted Quavers and Semiquavers
Staccato (Detached)

Dotted quavers and semiquavers played staccato (detached) are separated by a short pause, the bow however must NOT be lifted from the string.

These are generally played in one bow with a very crisp stroke of the wrist. Use upper half of bow. During the break between the two notes the bow is held pressed on the string.

Tramp! Tramp! Tramp!

George F. Root
1820–1895

Battle Hymn of the Republic

William Steffe

LESSON 31
Triplets

Triplets are groups of three notes played in the time of two notes of the same value. They are indicated by a figure ⌢3⌢ and a slur placed over or under a group of three notes.

A bar of 2/4 containing two triplets ♪♪♪♪♪♪ is the same as a bar of 6/8 in march time. 6/8 ♪♪♪♪♪♪

Pilgrims' Chorus
(Tannhäuser)

Richard Wagner
1813-1883

Alla Breve or 2/2 Time

Alla Breve, or cut time ¢ is played the same as 2/4 time. Each note having half the value as in 4/4 time, a minim being the unit of a beat.

Softly Now The Light of Day

von Weber

German College Song

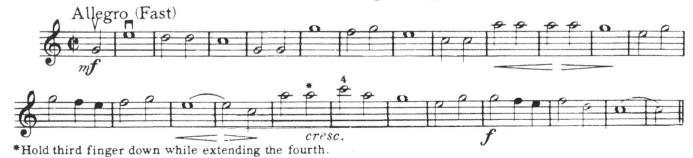

*Hold third finger down while extending the fourth.

LESSON 32
Staccato Bowing

Staccato, meaning detached, separated, is a style of bowing used in violin playing to denote a short crisp note. Notes to be played staccato are marked with a dot, placed over or under them. Draw the bow with a short, quick stroke, and then suddenly stopping it for a short rest, during which the bow is pressed firmly on the string. With this stroke the vibration of the string is stopped which gives the short staccato effect.

Andante
from Surprise Symphony

Haydn

Chromatics

The word "chromatic" means moving by semitones. Chromatic (literally, coloured) is well chosen, for by the use of sharps and flats, tone colour or shading is added to the natural sounds of the notes. A chromatic interval is one semitone above or below the given note. A chromatic scale is a scale that ascends or descends by semitones. In playing chromatics the finger must move quickly to the new note so that no slide is heard.

Etude

Wohlfahrt

Pizzicato

Pizz. means to pluck the string. The bow is held against the palm of the hand by the second, third and fourth fingers, the first being free to do the plucking. The tip of the thumb is placed against the corner of the fingerboard under the E string.

Amaryllis

Henri Ghys

LESSON 33

Sweet and Low
Quartet

Joseph Barnby
1838-1896

LESSON 34
From the Classics

Theme From the Violin Concerto

Beethoven

Theme From Symphony No.1

Brahms

Allegro non troppo (Not too fast)

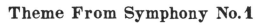

Theme From Der Freischütz

von Weber

Theme From Symphony No. 8

Beethoven

Printed by Printwise (Haverhill) Limited, Suffolk   10/09 (171659)